A TURTLE'S GUIDE TO INTROVERSION

縮頭龜的逆襲

BY TON MAK

鄭煥昇—譯

CHRONICLE BOOKS

SAN FRANCISCO

如果你是內向者，這本是你的書，你會在每一頁的烏龜獨白中找到自己；

如果你是外向者，這本是把鑰匙，可以打開你通往陌生世界的一扇窗，

幫助你認識、了解那群看起來神祕、毫不在乎、甚至有點反社會的人；

如果你不確定自己是內向還是外向，其實也不用急著找答案，慢慢地、

用自己的步調看這本書，你會有些頭緒。

沒有什麼龜息大法或龜派氣功，Ton Mak 的這隻烏龜就是內向者本來的

樣子，希望你也可以從書中找到屬於自己的寧靜。

———張瀞仁／美國 Give2Asia's 基金會家族慈善主任

「特殊狀況下，我真的很希望能躲進盒子裡。」內向的小龜縮回殼裡的樣子，根本就是我在滿溢著陌生人的場合中的模樣──恨不得把自己摺好、收進盒子裡原地休眠（要解散的時候再叫我，謝囉）。

過去我們認為「內向」就是害羞、在人前不敢說話，但現在更常見的說法是，內向與外向的差異在於這兩類人獲得能量的方法。內向的人不一定無法與人社交，但是比起社交，他們在獨處的時候更快樂或滿足。

對我來說，把時間和精力留給摯友、留給自己，當個快樂的宅宅是最棒的事了。就像小龜可以大方地淡出社交場合，現在的我被問到週末有什麼約，也會毫不勉強自己地回答：「沒有，但是我不想出門。」

──刷比／圖文創作者

內向的我們，常常覺得社交是一件疲乏的事，有時也會很想躲進屬於自己的小空間。

不過，慢慢來也沒關係，照著自己喜歡的步調走，享受一個人獨處的時光、也享受適當且舒服的交友圈。雖然我們很慢熟，但只要熟起來，都是很重要的好朋友。

作者可愛的插圖配上簡單而中肯的文字，句句寫進心坎裡，是一本很療癒、很放鬆的書，心中彷彿獲得了暖暖的能量。

———啊宣 ASUAN ／圖文作家

要記得，你永遠可以選擇讓自己更快樂、更舒心的方式生活。理解自己的喜好和厭惡、知道自己什麼時候要休息、要往哪個方向前進。縮頭烏龜不是膽小也不是逃避，而是徹徹底底地了解自己。

——— LuckyLulu／圖文作家

僅以本書獻給我的父親，多明尼克。

This book is dedicated to my father, Dominic.

我是小龜。

I am Turtle.

我想我是隻內向的烏龜。

I believe I may be an introvert.

偶爾，社交會讓我覺得有點疲乏。

Sometimes, socializing can feel a bit draining.

我不太知道該說什麼好……

It's hard to know the right thing to say . . .

也抓不準開口的時機。

or the right time to say it.

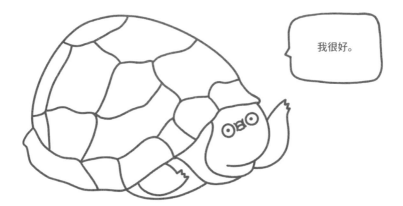

我很好。

特殊狀況下，我真的很希望能躲進盒子裡。

In certain situations, I really wish
I could hide in a box.

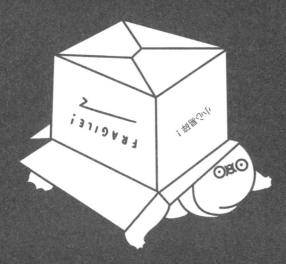

我超享受自己的陪伴。

I deeply enjoy my own company.

我最帶勁的時候，就是沒有人吵我、一個人
想東想西的時候。

I feel energized when I am on my own,
with my own thoughts.

～三個小時後～
3 hours later

我很納悶基努李維
今年幾歲了啊……

我喜歡散那種很長很長、很慢很慢的步……

I enjoy long, slow walks . . .

邊散步邊逃離社交場合。

away from social situations.

在忙嗎！

閒聊不是我的菜。

不是因為我不愛交朋友，或是討厭
跟人說話──而是單純因為閒聊感覺
像是為了聊而聊。

I don't like small talk.

Not because I am unfriendly or dislike conversations—but simply
because it feels
sort of forced sometimes.

超市結帳隊伍中的對話
讓我輕微地感到焦慮。

Conversations in the supermarket
checkout line give me mild anxiety.

呃……

但看到麻吉跟

家人，我會想知道他們的近況。

But when I see my close friends and family,
I enjoy catching up.

我會試著挖掘表面之下的東西。
I try to go beyond the surface.

我會樂於傾聽他們的新發想……
I like to hear about their new ideas . . .

思緒……
thoughts . . .

與感受。
and feelings.

我喜歡吸收並解讀
別人說的話。

I enjoy absorbing and interpreting
what the other person is saying.

有意義的互動讓人格外滿足。

Meaningful interactions are the most fulfilling.

而當有人禮尚往來地
也願意當我的聽眾，我的心也會
一點一點打開。

And when someone listens to
me in return, my heart begins
to open up too.

我可能會慢慢地分享
自己的感受，一筆接著一筆。

I may slowly start to share my feelings,
one by one.

朋友之間有時候無聲勝有聲。

Companionable silences are great sometimes.

光坐在一起就是一種享受。

最好還有吃的。

It can be nice to simply sit together
with some grub.

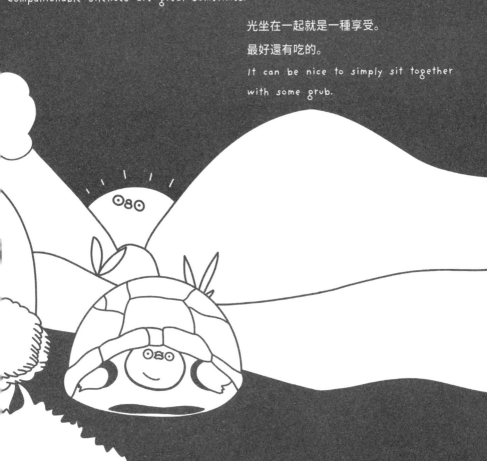

我喜歡把僅有的社交能量

保留給跟我比較麻吉的那一群。

I like to reserve my energy for socializing with
a more intimate group.

更進一步說，我想把精力留給自己。

And above all, I love reserving energy for myself.

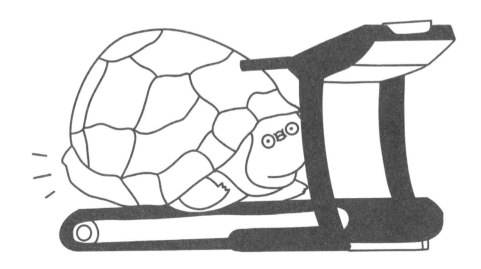

所以你知道，我熱愛獨處

在我有著拱頂的龜殼裡。

You see, I love being alone
in my domed shell.

我今天可忙了。

～五個小時後～
5 hours later

身為一隻內向的烏龜，最吸引人的是我

內心世界的思緒與感情。

Being an introvert, I am drawn to my inner world of thoughts and feelings.

我可以坐著納悶各種事情……

I can sit around wondering about things . . .

想像不同的情境……

回想過往的記憶……

規劃將來的人生大計。

imagining different scenarios . . .

recalling events from the past . . .

and making plans for the future.

一場精采的白日夢，可以有效
點燃我的想像力。

A good daydream can really
spark the imagination.

我可以當個宅宅。

I can be a homebody.

家是我的避風港。

My home is my safe place.

很多日常的活動，都讓我

覺得很有趣，比方說：

I find many everyday activities quite fun,
such as:

種種花草。

Potting plants.

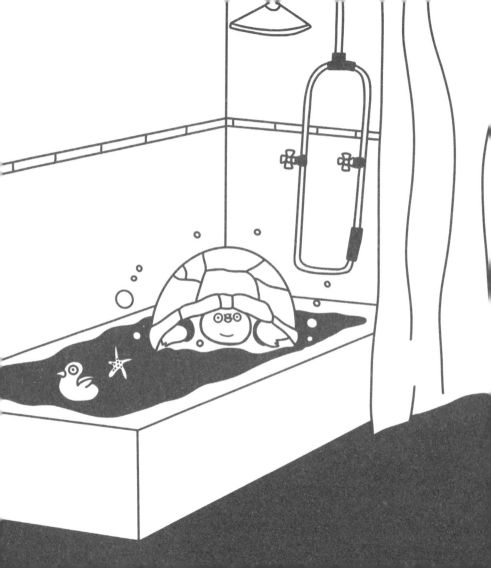

在浴缸裡深呼吸。

Deep breathing in a bathtub.

跟軟綿綿的動物當玩伴。

Playing with soft animals.

瞪著熔岩燈看。

Staring into a lava lamp.

深度的專注與全副的注意力

可以讓尋常的事物大變身。

Deep focus and full attention can turn
an ordinary object into an extraordinary one.

我很享受從事跟創意、
哲理，還有心靈有關係的活動。

I find enjoyment in creative, philosophical,
and spiritual endeavors.

自己忙自己的讓我渾身是勁。

I feel empowered to do things on my own.

我喜歡藝術創作……

I enjoy making art . . .

喜歡聽音樂······

listening to music . . .

喜歡親近大自然。

or spending time in nature.

獨處有助於我按下暫停鍵
休息一會兒。

Time alone helps me pause
for a moment and reset.

我可以靜下心來
單純地處於當下。

I can still my mind
and just be present.

我會設法不讓自己淹沒

於外在世界的喧囂中。

I try not to feel overwhelmed

by the noise of the external world.

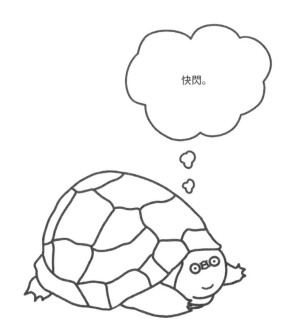

快閃。

但若真的感覺到天旋地轉，

我仍可以回歸自己的內在。

But when I do feel overwhelmed,
I can turn inward.

有時候我的聲音會消失

在偌大的辦公室環境中。

Sometimes my voice gets lost
in large office environments.

三不五時，

我寧可單機作業。

Every now and then,
I prefer working alone.

個人空間是我生產力的根源。

Personal space is vital to my productivity.

在享有獨立空間，想法與創意不受打擾的地方，
我才能全力衝刺。

I work best when I can be independent,
left alone with my thoughts and ideas.

獨處，可以是創新的催化劑。

Solitude can be a catalyst to innovation.

身邊的人可能說話比我快，
音量比我大，氣勢比我強。

Others around me may speak faster,
louder, and with more confidence.

但我不應該就此覺得自己要跟他們比快。

其他人或許嗓門大些，但我的意見也同樣有價值 。

But I shouldn't feel like I need to hurry.
Others may be louder, but my ideas are just as valid.

我一直在想……

要用自己的方法，那不代表我做錯了啥。

I like to share my ideas in my own way, and that's OK.

內向者很容易被人誤會。

Introverts can be easily misunderstood.

哇嗚，你看了
一整天的雲耶。

旁人可能會想當然耳地以為
我反社會。

Others may incorrectly assume
that I am antisocial.

但我不會把這些誤解放在心上。

內向是我力量的來源。

But I don't let their opinions bother me.

Being introverted is a source of power.

夥伴。

別當隻難搞的烏龜。

我自有一套

處理問題的辦法……

I have adopted my own ways

of dealing with problems . . .

包括借助靜坐
through meditating . . .

借助音樂
through music . . .

借助獨處
through alone time . . .

借助白日夢
through daydreaming . . .

也借助有創意的表達。
and through creative expression.

我無時無刻不在嘗試表達
自己的感受……

I am constantly trying to
express my feelings . . .

我不想把這些感受悶在心頭
直到它們最後像火山一樣爆發。

without bottling them up
until they explode like a volcano.

我喜歡慢慢地理解、消化周遭世界。

I enjoy digesting the world around me slowly.

我會傾聽自己的身體，
還有自己的心。

I listen to my body
and my heart.

我會忠於自己的本性，給自己充分的時間去消化跟紓壓。

I stay true to my nature, and give myself the time I need to digest and decompress.

不同人的筆順會不同。

Different strokes for different folks.

但都應該受到尊重。

And that's OK.

內向是我的超能力。
Introversion is a great strength.

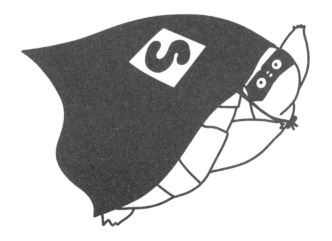

也是我的私房醬料……
說不定也是你的。

It's my secret sauce . . .
and perhaps it's yours too.

尾聲的一點龜派小語……

Some final turtle words . . .

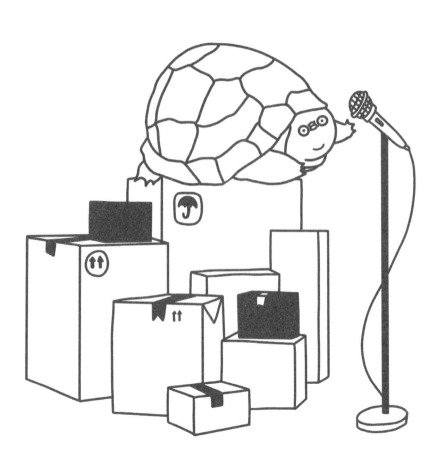

記得要給自己充足的時間
去找到自己的聲音。

Be sure to give yourself all the time
you need to find your voice.

不用在意自己比較慢熱……

It's OK to share slowly . . .

比較溫吞。

and quietly.

不是非得用吼的，才叫作自信。
Confidence doesn't always roar.

有時候有些自信的展現
可能沒那麼吵鬧，沒那麼招搖。
Sometimes, it can be expressed
in quieter and subtler forms.

力量與勇氣

常在你心。

There is strength and courage
already in your heart.

非常有可能……
它們一直都沒有離開過你。

Most likely . . .
it's been there all along.

還有別忘記，永遠要忠於自己。

And remember, always stay true to yourself.

那個有些地方很美好、有些地方怪怪的自己。

The wonderful bits and the weird.

*Fun系列*079

縮頭龜的逆襲：當內向是種天性，做自己就是義務！
A Turtle's Guide to Introversion

圖‧文：Ton Mak｜譯者：鄭煥昇｜主編：陳家仁｜編輯：黃凱怡｜企劃：藍秋惠｜美術設計：陳恩安｜總編輯：胡金倫｜董事長：趙政岷｜出版者：時報文化出版企業股份有限公司／108019台北市和平西路三段240號4樓／發行專線：02-2306-6842／讀者服務專線：0800-231-705；02-2304-7103／讀者服務傳真：02-2304-6858／郵撥：19344724時報文化出版公司／信箱：10899臺北華江橋郵政第99信箱／時報悅讀網：www.readingtimes.com.tw｜法律顧問：理律法律事務所／陳長文律師、李念祖律師｜印刷：華展印刷有限公司｜初版一刷：2021年4月9日｜定價：新台幣360元｜版權所有　翻印必究（缺頁或破損的書，請寄回更換）

ISBN 978-957-13-8809-0｜Printed in Taiwan

時報文化出版公司成立於一九七五年，並於一九九九年股票上櫃公開發行，
於二〇〇八年脫離中時集團非屬旺中，以「尊重智慧與創意的文化事業」為信念。

縮頭龜的逆襲：當內向是種天性，做自己就是義務！／Ton Mak圖.文；鄭煥昇譯. -- 初版. -- 臺北市：時報文化出版企業股份有限公司，2021.04；128面；15×15公分. --（Fun；79）｜中英對照｜譯自：A turtle's guide to introversion.｜ISBN 978-957-13-8809-0（平裝）｜1.內向性格 2.自我肯定 3.生活指導｜173.73｜110003885